A Guru
In The Nursery

DAWN M· STASZAK

A Guru
In The Nursery

50 Ways to Remember Your
Spirit While Changing Diapers

BALBOA.
PRESS
A DIVISION OF HAY HOUSE

Balboa Press books may be ordered through booksellers or by contacting:

Balboa Press
A Division of Hay House
1663 Liberty Drive
Bloomington, IN 47403
www.balboapress.com
1-(877) 407-4847

Because of the dynamic nature of the Internet, any web addresses or links contained in this book may have changed since publication and may no longer be valid. The views expressed in this work are solely those of the author and do not necessarily reflect the views of the publisher, and the publisher hereby disclaims any responsibility for them.

The author of this book does not dispense medical advice or prescribe the use of any technique as a form of treatment for physical, emotional, or medical problems without the advice of a physician, either directly or indirectly. The intent of the author is only to offer information of a general nature to help you in your quest for emotional and spiritual well-being. In the event you use any of the information in this book for yourself, which is your constitutional right, the author and the publisher assume no responsibility for your actions.

Any people depicted in stock imagery provided by Thinkstock are models, and such images are being used for illustrative purposes only. Certain stock imagery © Thinkstock.

Printed in the United States of America

ISBN: 978-1-4525-6587-3 (sc)
ISBN: 978-1-4525-6589-7 (hc)
ISBN: 978-1-4525-6588-0 (e)

Library of Congress Control Number: 2012923888

Balboa Press rev. date: 1/03/2012

Dedication

I dedicate this book to my children,
William Alexander
&
Victoria Elizabeth

Mommy loves you!

About the Author

DAWN M. STASZAK IS the author of two previous books, "A Guru In The Office," and "A Fish Out Of Water," and proud mother of a preschooler and a toddler, William and Victoria, respectively.

As of this writing, she is the Small Wonders Facilitator (presenting Science of Mind© principles in lessons and stories for ages 0-4) at her church, DuPage Center for Spiritual Living, and Mom-Tot Coordinator for the Chicago Western Suburban Chapter of the Holistic Moms Network.

Her interest in all things metaphysical began in early childhood, but she specifically began studying and researching all New Thought wisdom since the early 1990s. She is currently living in Aurora, Illinois with her husband, Chris, the kids, and their two cats.

"... One of his most precious teachings is that we may equally court the Presence in deep prayer or while washing dishes at the kitchen sink.

... Discovering the sacred within all moments is the fruitage of spiritual awakening. In other words, our everyday life is not a distraction from our formal spiritual practices of meditation and affirmative prayer. There is no division between the sacred and the mundane."

Dr. Michael Bernard Beckwith, w/Anita Rehker from Science of Mind Magazine, November, 2010 Issue, page 10, "The Mystical Threads That Bind," article, speaking of Carmelite monk, Brother Lawrence.

Table of Contents

Preface

FIRST AND FOREMOST, I want to make it absolutely clear that I am in no way declaring *myself* a "Guru" of being a Mother. I had my opinions and judgments before I became a Mother, and boy, have I been eating my words. I have, at times, never been happier or more miserable than I have been since giving birth. I am still learning. This book is only to share with other Moms some tips on how I got through the toughest times thus far.

Secondly, I want to make it clear that everything I say here and in the following pages is simply my opinion and not meant to be a judgment if someone does or believes something different.

Finally, I am not comparing myself to anyone. As of this writing, I cannot speak for or know what it is like to be a single Mom, a divorced Mom, or a part-time working Mom. I can only write about what I know.

In my case, I was a Working Mom of a 1½ year old, but became a Stay-At-Home-Mom when I found out I was pregnant with my second child. Being at home was so much harder than I thought it would be only having my toddler to look after…and then I had my newborn and discovered exactly how much harder it could get! Things got completely out of control. That is why I needed to figure out how in the world I was going to do this. How could I best care for my children, keep my sanity, try to manage my stress, and maintain my spirituality at the same time? Well, I didn't for a while. I completely lost it. I chronicled my thoughts, feelings, and humorous anecdotes on it all in a blog titled "A Fish Out of Water," which then became my second book.

Whether you bring in a paycheck or not, being a Mother is the most blessed, sacred responsibility you will ever have. If I have learned anything it is this: It is of the utmost importance you care for yourself in order to care for your child(ren). The following pages describe ways I have discovered to not only cope, but thrive, in the most trying days of Motherhood – the diaper years. This is the time in which your children are most vulnerable, and so are you.

When reading, please note that I began writing this book while pregnant with my daughter and my son had just turned two. As of this publication, my daughter just turned two and my son is now four. This is why you may see that I refer to my children anywhere between the ages of newborn to four.

Also, throughout this book you will see the word "Mom" in capital letters. This is done on purpose because I have come to realize that the title deserves such respect. Although I have never known such joy, I have never worked so hard in my entire life. Also, you will see the acronym "SAHM" which stands for "Stay-At-Home-Mom."

If you are lucky enough to have a staff of people around you to help, such as a cook, maid, and nanny, then you probably don't need this book. For most of us who don't, however, we need to find that inner strength to get through the day, connect with our Source, feel fulfillment in being a parent, and feel happiness in being with our beautiful child(ren) when ultimately, we are their primary caregivers.

Being at home can be very lonely, especially when you only have one child to talk to, if they are even talking at all yet. I am still reeling at how hard it was in the beginning to get both my children dressed and out of the house most days (much less myself), and I am in awe of how I ever found the strength to do it, but I did. I can only credit the Source for giving me the strength and determination to figure all this out – which is why I needed to write this book. I really needed this information and I am sure I'm not the only one, so I was inspired to share it with other new Moms in the hopes it could help them in the way it helped me.

In building my network of other SAHMs, I learned I was by far not the only one who felt this way. In fact, I learned of other SAHMs who were in even worse shape because they either had post-partum depression or alcoholism issues. As with the first book, I needed to write this book for me, but also, with the hope that it helps anyone else out there who finds themselves in this situation. You may be by yourself, but you are not alone.

We worry so much about doing the right thing for our children and what influences the world will have on them. The bottom line is that no matter what friends they have, what the experts say, what the teachers say, or what they watch on TV, you are the parent and what goes on in the home is the foundation through which they filter the world. As long as you do your best and be their best support through the good times and bad, loving them to the best of your ability throughout, you will have done your job well.

Most importantly, know and remember God is there for you. These are the things that helped me regain a sense of balance and connection to Spirit when I felt completely out of control and lost. My hope is that these tips help you as well.

All of this is meant to remind you that, in fact, you are your own "guru."

Acknowledgements

I WANT TO ACKNOWLEDGE the many people who have helped me tremendously in the creation of this book, which include my family, my friends, and my "cheerleaders," for their emotional support, advice, and information. Specifically, a big "thank you" from the bottom of my heart to...

My Husband, Chris Staszak, for all his support, including being an excellent Father; and his technical assistance with the manuscript drafts.

My Mother, Florence Lacey, for her endless examples of selfless devotion and teaching me what it means to be a loving parent; and especially for her dozens of hours of babysitting while I worked on this book!

My "Gurls," for their emotional support and loving friendship for over 20 years and still going strong: Colleen Anderson, Kim Brakeall, Amy Christiansen, Koreen Engstrom, Janet Jackson, Sarah Kulikowski, Gretta Nelson, Nancy Ramirez, Jenny Rammacher, Yolanda Rodriguez, Bridget Stuart, Launetta "Elle" Thompson, Jade Walker, Kelly Williams, and Jean Wray. Your unending support and listening ears are worth more than gold.

My "Spiritual Support Team," Revs. Mary Beth and Michael Speer, Rev. Mary Hermann, Rev. Kathy Kuna, Rev. Kathy Mertes, Rev. Jean Miner, Lori Brogan, Donna Damato, Auriel Grace, Deb Hanneman, Kevin Matti, and Darlene Palese.

My "Church Mom" friends, Pam Asa and Missy McDonald. Pam, for having her wonderful daughter, Natalie, relieve me from my lessons from time-to-time so I can experience the service. Missy, for having her adorable baby participate in my program.

My friend, Genis Schmidt, for turning me on to and participating with me in Spiritual activities for our kids.

My friend, Diana Kloster, for turning me onto, advising me, and supporting me in my Turbofire® program, which has helped me tremendously; including being there in a pinch to watch the kids that time, as well as her overall loyal support and friendship.

My neighbor, Rashida Pflipsen, for being a wonderful friend, supporter, and confidant, and for doing the "kid swap" days with me when I really needed it!

My neighbor, Debbie Nies for watching the kids for me when I had appointments and speaking engagements and being a wonderful friend.

My friend, Angie Kershaw, for being a fantastic child care provider and taking great care of my kids when I needed her…and for being my "all things 80's" soul-sister!

My friend, Cherie Denton, for generously offering her time and talent with last-minute editing.

All the wonderful Moms in my Holistic Moms Network for their wisdom, support, encouragement, time, and a listening ear.

Last, but not least, I thank my entire Facebook family for their unending support and friendship!

I am so incredibly blessed to have each and every one of you in my life!

Section One
Daily Life

HERE ARE SOME EASY ways to incorporate your spirituality into your day – some even without having to take up any extra time! These are presented chronologically throughout your day to show you how to do this from the time your feet touch the floor until your head rests on the pillow again.

An Attitude of Gratitude

First and foremost, begin your day with gratitude – gratitude for your baby(ies) being born in this world and for you being their Mom. There are lessons only you can teach them, because every Mom is different. Whether you are at home, working outside the home, on the road, traditionally educated, or street-smart, your children will learn from you.

There are so many people out there who are trying to get pregnant and/or adopt children. I didn't understand why it was considered a "miracle" to get pregnant (since there are billions of people in the world) – until it happened to me.

Yet, when they are finally here and if you happen to have a baby with colic or a disability, it can (at times) be extremely difficult to find gratitude for the situation. I had to work hard to find the strength to change my thinking, compose some affirmations, and find some positive people to snap myself back into the realization of the wonderful blessing I had – even through the crying and vomiting episodes!

Constantly saying to yourself how hard it is does nothing but confirm it. Remind yourself that this situation is fleeting. They will all-too-soon grow up to become children, teenagers, and then adults. Look into their eyes and upon them as they sleep, and feel the love and gratitude pouring from your heart. It is healing to both them and you.

Prayer

HONESTLY, SOMETIMES THE ONLY thing that got me through the day in the first few months after my second child was born was to just stop for a minute and pray. I recall once when they both happened to be sleeping at the same time, I got down on my knees out of pure gratitude for even just a moment's peace.

I prayed for strength, I prayed to get through the day, and I prayed to be present for my child(ren) and spouse. It wasn't long, just a few seconds to speak aloud or simply think the thoughts that were in my head. I found that whispering them aloud was helpful to get them out so I could hear them for myself. It made me feel better and snapped me back into a clearer frame of mind.

I like the idea of using prayer to get my children in the habit of focusing on their good and where it comes from – the Source of all good. I do my best to remember to say a simple prayer of gratitude with the kids before eating a meal (usually dinner), and especially when I find good parking spots.

Also, instead of saying the old "Now I Lay Me Down to Sleep," at bedtime, I basically run down a simple "gratitude list" of their own. After lights are out, and I'm either lying or sitting beside my toddler in bed, I take a few moments to review his day with him to teach him gratitude for everything good that happened that day and all the good things he has in his life (Mommy, Daddy, Sister, pets, food, bed, etc.) This is to try and ensure he has good thoughts in his head while entering sleep.

Then, I do the same for myself. When I can, before I go to bed, I do my best to journal, or at least review in my mind all the good that happened during the day and everything I have to be grateful for in my life. Every night I read a Daily Guide from my *Science of Mind* magazine, and either one or more of the following: a passage from *Awakenings* by Shakti Gawain, affirmation cards (either ones that I've made or from Louise Hay), "Angel Cards," inspirational cards from Wayne Dyer or the Dalai Lama, or my intentions. Any and all of this is to impress good thoughts into my subconscious before entering sleep, which I find helps me sleep better (for as long as that may be).

Cleansing Visualization

SHOWERING IS SOMETHING WE all must do (even as hard as it is with having a newborn!), so I use it as another opportunity to practice one of my favorite secret tricks because it takes up no extra time. It is simply all visualization.

When I take a shower, I use it as an opportunity to cleanse my energy and thoughts as well. I imagine the water as a magical shimmering liquid that is penetrating my body and washing away all the dark negativity down the drain. Therefore, I end the shower feeling cleansed both inside and out.

Order

BEFORE MY SECOND BABY arrived and I became a Stay-At-Home Mom, my goal was to clean out as much as I could from my home and then find a place for everything so I could keep a simple, tidy, and orderly living space for all of us. I had a hard enough time keeping things clean and in place with just my 1½ year old, and I knew that when the baby came, it was going to be near impossible.

To be peaceful, I must have my mind and physical surroundings clear and orderly. Fortunately, we were able to keep our toddler in day care for two more weeks while I went through each room of my home and cleaned out things. If possible (when you are feeling up to it), have someone watch baby for at least two hours at a time to clear away and organize what is always visible to you. It eases tension not to have to worry about that clutter on the counter or if you really need that many plastic containers in your cupboard. Allow for kids' messes and freedom, but at the end of the day (or even once a week, whatever works for you!), clear it away. I've discovered clear plastic sandwich and snack bags work wonders for keeping together small toys, such as plastic trinkets, memory cards, and magnets!

Another thing that has really helped is keeping the diaper bag in order, especially after I had my second child. My husband came up with the brilliant idea of using our backpack as a diaper bag, so that I could organize things into different pockets and also so that the weight of the bag would be positioned evenly across my back. The small pocket in the front is for the "medicinal" items such as thermometer, lotion, nail file, band-aids, "After-Bite" and the like. The first large pocket is for the diapers, wipes, rash cream, and changing pad. The middle pocket is for food items such as the baby's bottles and formula, care log and pen, bibs, burp cloths, toddler's snacks, and his water bottle. The back pocket is for extra clothes for each child, a blanket, some toys and rattles, and a plastic bag for dirty clothes. One side pocket is for extra granola bars for Mommy and my bag checklist. The other side pocket is for hand sanitizer, napkins, Kleenex, and sunglasses. As long as I had this bag packed, I was gold. Of course, I looked like I was going on some kind of mountain hike, but at least I had peace of mind!

Family Calendar

I GOT THE IDEA from an article to create a family meal/activity calendar to display on the fridge for all to see. It is an 11" x 14" erasable whiteboard calendar with the days of the week already on it. I'm sure you can find it at any local store in the office supply aisle.

Each month all I have to do is put the name of the month on top and the dates. I use a different colored dry-erase marker each month for fun. Then, I put down what I plan to make each day of the week. For instance, Monday would be "Fish," Tuesday is "Pasta," Wednesday "Chicken," and Saturday is always homemade "Pizza" night. On Sundays in the summer it's always "Grill" (my husband's department) and in the winter it's "Slow-Cooker" or "Casserole," so that we have leftovers for Mondays (to make Mondays that much easier).

Although I do this each month, it is not set in stone, it is just nice for me to have it all laid out to give me somewhat of a plan and then I can tweak it as I like. In doing this, it's one less thing to have as a stressor – to alleviate the dreaded "What's for dinner?" question all the time. As I review each meal planned, I give thanks that we are so blessed to have food to eat every day and to know that we intend to have food to eat in the coming month.

So, not only do we knock out the question of what is for dinner, but I also put down whatever important plans we have going on, such as doctor's appointments, kids' classes, evening dates, weekend events, or family visits for holidays and birthdays and the like. This way, everyone knows what's going on. To bring this to the current times, my husband and I also have an application on our phone where we can share calendars, so I mainly use the one on the refrigerator for meals, but also, it's nice to have the "at-a-glance" convenience for the entire family. Plus, as I go through the events of the coming month at the beginning of the month, it is nice for me to be able to look ahead, plan other activities, and get mentally prepared for it all. I intend to always use this as I imagine it will be even more crucial as the kids get older and have their own schedules going on.

Housework

OKAY, YOU'RE THINKING, "How can housework be spiritual?" I don't mean the "cleanliness next to Godliness" thing here, either. It's not the task, but it's how you go about it.

First, express gratitude for having a home to clean in the first place, when so many people in this world do not. Look around your home and say, "What a gorgeous home! I am so grateful for this place! We are so lucky to have a wonderful home such as this to eat in, sleep in, and play in! Thank you, Lord!"

Second, use non-toxic products to clean your home as much as possible. To purchase, some of them may cost a little more, but better yet, you can make your own. Baking soda and water make a simple paste to clean the bathtub and toilets. Liquid detergent and vinegar make a great window cleaner. Olive oil and lemon juice make a nice furniture polish. There is an abundance of information available on the internet, such as at www.about.com, but a great book to read for starters is "Organic Housecleaning," by Ellen Sandbeck. Otherwise, just do a "Goodsearch" (www. goodsearch.com) on "natural cleaning" and you'll find how to use the items I listed above such as vinegar, lemon juice, and baking soda to clean just about anything from toilets to floors to the kitchen sink and everything in between.

Third, find a cleaning schedule or system that works for you and put any accomplishments in a planner so you can track what you've done and know when it's time to do it again. I found that About.com (mentioned above) was not only a great resource for using natural products, but also for home cleaning schedules – it has a daily, weekly, monthly, and seasonal cleaning schedule.

To start, I tried to do the "one room at a time" method and it just didn't work for me. I've tried to do certain rooms on certain days, and that didn't work for me either. Ultimately, however, I discovered that when I wanted to vacuum, I preferred to vacuum every room. When I wanted to do the mirrors, it was easier to simply do the mirrors in every room. Voila! I discovered a system for myself. Now, the problem was time.

Time is always an issue when you are a parent, and especially having to get anything done in the home while toddlers are around. I found just about the only thing that worked for me while I still had a baby was to get my Mom to watch the kids while I cleaned. This is because every time I tried to clean, I realized I wasn't watching my children. No big surprise. They just weren't of age to "play by themselves," being newborn and two. I was able to clean when I only had my then 1½-year-old, because he could watch his "Your Baby Can Read" videos which gave me some time (and without the guilt that he was watching something mindless). Plus, I could clean while he napped. With a baby and a toddler, however, the naps just don't coordinate on a regular basis, and thus, I needed the extra help. When they were older (3 and 1), I was able to hire a dear friend's teenage daughter during the summer to watch them for a couple of hours a week while I cleaned – at half the price of a regular sitter! – it was a win-win situation!

So, the point in sharing all this with you is to encourage you to find what works for you. That means also working on getting help any way you can, championing your efforts, and feeling gratitude for what you have. Connecting with Spirit isn't just about going to church, but also when you are doing the "mundane" tasks in life, such as housework. If you can pray while cleaning house, you've got it!

Mindful Living

I DO MY BEST to be environmentally conscious. Not only is it an ethical practice for humanity and my children, but it is practical as well because it cuts down on waste and clutter.

One way I do this is that I happily take hand-me-down clothes for my kids from my sister and friends, and then I give back, donate, or sell what I no longer need.

An important choice we've made (even before we had kids) is that our family owns nothing but hybrid vehicles. We purchased our Prius in 2005 and we have saved thousands on gas and oil changes – I can even prove it because my husband keeps a spreadsheet! We bought a Ford Escape Hybrid when my son came along.

Another way to live mindfully is to take a good look at how your family eats and where you get your food. We typically only eat red meat on Sundays during "grilling season," if that. Otherwise, I do my best to have my family eat fish, pasta, soups, turkey, and chicken. If your family enjoys meat, a good resource is to find a CSA (Community Supported Agriculture) group. It is a wonderful resource to connect you directly with local food sources to support local economy and consume natural, high-quality foods. Also, be on the lookout for farmer's markets, which are becoming more available as demand grows. The kids love to visit them during the summer!

On the subject of food, that includes how and what you are feeding your baby. I breastfed for the first eight months of both babies' lives, and then when it came time for solids, I made their own food. It wasn't as hard as people think – I just mashed up stuff! I am no cook, so that was doable for me; I could mash up stuff no problem! I understand that breastfeeding is a hot topic at the moment, so I am not here to judge either way. I did both breast and bottle and my kids are fine.

I would suggest that if you are able to breastfeed, it sure is convenient because it saves hundreds of dollars on formula, you never have to worry about being without, and it is the healthier, natural alternative. When I nursed each of my babies, I truly felt a deep connection to them and to Spirit, the whole web of life, and being a part of the natural design. Yet, if you can't or don't want to breastfeed, that choice deserves to be respected and don't let anyone tell you any different. I include that option here mainly in the interest of mindful living.

Aside from what I put into my body and my family's bodies, I do my best to take a good look at what I put on them as well. On my baby registry, I made sure to choose bath products and accessories from the "green" or "natural" sections. I was thrilled to discover that Wal-Mart has a "green" products area in their bath and body section, too, so I am able to purchase "Burt's Bees" products there to bathe and lotion my kids.

Another way I discovered to be "green," is to recycle my cards. Every year I get beautiful holiday and birthday cards. It means a lot to me, so I have a hard time throwing them in the recycling bin, but when I used to keep them all, it really piled up over the years. Then, I found a solution! A friend turned me on to the St. Jude's Ranch for card recycling where I can mail them my cards. Now, I simply keep the cards for just one year and when I get new ones, I put the photo cards in a photo album, and donate the previous year's paper cards, which is a good compromise for a "pack rat" like me! Visit http://www.stjudesranch.org/shop/recycled-card-program/ for details on how to participate.

Another very easy way to give back is to "shop to support;" that is, get a credit card that gives a portion to charity, such as the World Wildlife Fund. Visit www.worldwildlife.org, "How to Help" tab, then "Shop to Support" link. Search the internet for other causes near and dear to your heart and you may find other credit cards or purchase programs to support them as well, all by doing something we all must do eventually – shop!

Finally, as part of living mindfully, I do my best to use only green/non-toxic cleaning products, as mentioned in the previous chapter on "Housework."

There are several other lifestyle choices you can make to live mindfully and sustainably, such as composting, shopping with reusable bags, and using LCD light bulbs. Please visit www.earth911.com for more ideas.

Stay Active

SIGN YOUR BABY OR toddler up for at least one class a week for a session to get you both out of the house. It is important to do that as soon as it's safe for the baby because it is too easy to just stay home, since it is so overwhelming in the beginning. By getting out, you get to enjoy the weather (if possible) and meet others in your situation.

A great start is your local library. Aside from the hundreds of board books to choose from, most libraries have "lap sit" time for babies and story time for toddlers which involve not only the librarians reading books out loud, but also teaching them rhyming, songs, dances, and crafts. These library story times are free, educational, and provide an opportunity for you and your child to make new friends.

Another wonderful resource is your local park district. The classes are reasonably-priced, particularly if you are a resident within the park district boundaries, and they offer seasonal one-time events as well.

Three months after I had my daughter, I registered my son and myself for a toddler/parent sports class. The park district has a day care to watch my baby for just $2 an hour, and I only needed the hour. It was important for me to do that with my son to let him know he was still my special little man, even though we have an addition to the family.

It was very, very difficult at first to get out of the house with both, but I forced myself to keep doing it for my sake and theirs, and I'm glad I did, because we would have missed out on a lot of fun if I hadn't.

Plus, I plan to do things like that on the weekends and evenings when I go back to work as well, because several of these programs are still available during those times. I was working when I had my son, and we took him to his "Aqua Tots" swim class on Saturday mornings after he turned one and it was a lot of fun.

Scheduling fun things is healthy because it keeps you all active and positive. Since childcare can be such a tough job, the more fun you have together, the better your relationship will be with your children and it is a great stress-reliever for you as well.

Fun and Learning

BE SURE TO SHARE joy with your child in any way possible – play, learn, read, watch. Have imaginative, non-electrical playtime with your toddler. When they are babies, the lights, buttons, and sounds help them learn cause and effect, colors, letters, words, and numbers. However, by the time they are toddlers, you will find you don't need those kinds of toys, because their imagination will bloom and that is the most entertaining and valuable playtime.

For example, my son could play for hours with plastic cups, balls, and water. I love to see him pretend that the living room is the "forest" and his Lightening McQueen tent is the "town" (he came up with these names on his own!). He also named his colored foam blocks in the corner of the basement his "garden" (I think because some were green with stripes that probably look like grass patches).

That said, I don't think that videos are a terrible thing in moderation. I needed my toddler to be in one place when the baby was born and I was breastfeeding. Yes, he ended up watching way more programs than I would have liked in the first three months, but eventually he got bored and got into the things he shouldn't, just as if I didn't have the program on in the first place. So he did not turn into an obese couch potato after all.

Interestingly enough, certain PBS and Netflix shows sparked his imagination even further. We were able to act out some scenarios that he saw, and then I used them as opportunities for learning certain values, such as sharing and manners. Reading was not only done by me, but reinforced by the "Your Baby Can Read" program, and the PBS programs "Word World" and "Super

Why." I was even able to introduce science to him thanks to "Sid the Science Kid," and we'd sing together about elasticity and gravity.

Before I became a Mom, I had all sorts of ideas of what I was going to do and what I should do, and believe me, having him watch TV programs was not in the plan. However, I have humbled myself plenty in these past couple of years! All the judgments, opinions, and ideas I had before I had kids have not entirely gone out the window, but have been modified, changed, and reconsidered now that I'm actually a Mom. Funny how that happens.

Therefore, just enjoy your children any way you can to the best of your ability, because this time is so fleeting. Don't forget to make having fun a priority. You'll be surprised at how much they can learn from simply playing with you.

Then, for the times when you need to get something else done and Daddy isn't home yet, don't beat yourself up for letting them watch something for a little bit, because you can always talk about what they've watched with them and teach them something from it to make it worthwhile and beneficial.

Music

CELEBRATE LIFE AND DANCE with your children! Dancing with babies, especially, is a good idea to help calm them and give them some fun play time. When children dance, they are getting good exercise, too, and it is a terrific stress reliever for all.

You can listen to "their" music (kids' tunes) or yours, or do a variety. Many children's CDs have educational value as well, such as counting rhymes and alphabet songs. This way, not only are you having fun with them, but teaching them as well.

Plus, I like to sing to my kids all the time. I made up special songs for each of them with their name in it as babies, and they smile and laugh when they recognize their name. I also introduced them to the "classics" such as "Somewhere Over the Rainbow" (which tends to relax my son) and "Tomorrow" (from "Annie"). Then, I find the corresponding videos on You Tube and show them to my toddler and he really enjoys that. When I first showed him the old 1960's Mickey Mouse Clubhouse "Mouseketeer" anthem he couldn't get enough of it!

In the morning, when I get the baby, I sing her a modified version of "Good Morning" from "Singin' in the Rain" that goes "Good morning, good morning … you slept the whole night through, good morning, good morning, to you and you and you!" and she loves it. William loved it, too, as a baby, so I figured I couldn't go wrong! Too bad they both didn't continue to "sleep the whole night through" now that they are toddlers!

Music heals, relaxes, and energizes – all depending on which harmonies you choose. One of my fondest childhood memories was on weekend mornings when my Mom would crank up the tunes on her huge stereo turntable and she'd dance with me and my sister. We had such fun and got good exercise, too. How wonderful it would be to create fun memories of your own for your kids!

There is a fantastic class series for kids ages 0-5 called "Music Together." It is an early childhood music program to teach them how to keep a beat, sing in tune, and introduce them to playing small instruments. I am blessed to have this program available through my library, but please visit www.musictogether.com to find a program near you.

Humor

EVERYONE KNOWS HUMOR IS the best stress reliever. In the movie, "The Secret," one lady even states that watching funny shows every day was part of the treatment she used to cure herself of breast cancer. I absolutely believe that positive energy increases healing endorphins in the body, and what better way to get there than laughter.

At my worst times, I had to laugh about some things or I would just cry (and, of course, I did that, too!). My unwitting comedic audience was my poor Facebook family, but heck, it kept me going! Facebook has been a source of great laughs for me, especially whenever I see those cards posted by www. someeecards.com. I have shared some of my own humorous observations in the Appendix section at the end of my second book, "A Fish Out of Water."

Of course, it is hard to laugh when your two-year-old has dumped all of the kitties' food into their water fountain (yes, lesson learned for Mommy not to leave it on the floor, despite the fact he's never touched it before) at the exact same time your newborn is screaming again…but, I figured if I took a picture of it with my phone and posted it on Facebook, then at least someone was sure to have a laugh, right?

Training your mind to find the humor and lightness in situations is truly a skill. However, it is a skill that will serve you and your family well in your daily lives and your toughest times versus the alternative. The alternative is not fun. I've been there and I don't like it at all. There is always a choice in which way to handle things.

If anything, when you are feeling at your worst, just smile. Smiling sends a "signal" to the brain to help lighten your mood. Try it, it works!

Inspiration in Commute

WHILE DRIVING THE KIDS to playdates, classes, or to the store, you can use this time to infuse your consciousness with positive thoughts that will stay with you throughout the day. When driving, try listening to relaxing music (as long as it doesn't make you sleepy, of course!), inspirational audio programs, or even church service recordings (my church provides CD recordings of their services for sale).

I especially enjoy my church's recordings because in the beginning it was very difficult for me to get to church as often as I liked. However, I purchased the past recordings to listen to whenever I was driving (usually on the way to or home from church) and I still get the benefits from it, even if I wasn't there that day.

However, I also really love listening to inspirational audio programs. Although it took several weeks, I was able to get through a large series, such as Paul Scheele's "Abundance for Life" program. On the other hand, it only took a couple of days for me to finish Louise Hay's "Embracing Change" CDs. Of course, I listen to my kids if they are talking to me and we hold conversations, so lots of times I repeat the CDs until I feel I've heard everything, but that's okay, because I know I am still getting something out of it. I enjoy it and it helps me, and that's what matters.

Afternoon Tea

I GOT INTO THE habit of having tea with my lunch, and it is a very nice treat. Having "tea time" makes me feel nice, like I'm pampering myself a little bit. It doesn't take any extra time out of my day either, since I still need to eat.

I enjoy either "Tazo" or "Yogi" brands. Tazo has great flavors, but I especially enjoy Yogi because it has special inspirational messages on the tea bag tags such as "Strength does not lie in what you have. It lies in what you can give." It's refreshing to receive an inspiring notion like that in the middle of a hectic day with the kids!

Feng Shui the Nursery

FENG SHUI IS THE ancient Chinese practice of furniture placement for optimal flow of energy ("chi"). It translates to "wind water." The point of this practice is to arrange the location of objects in the room for the best energy flow in order to manifest prosperity and good health. Who doesn't want that for their children?

If you can, I believe it is worth it to hire a trained consultant not only to do the baby's room, but also to do the rest of the home as well. Although I own and have studied several books on the subject, I discovered that it is a definite art which would take years of training to fully know, such as Astrology, Reflexology, or Herbalism.

If you'd prefer not to spend the money then you can look it up at the library or else just browse the internet from the comfort of your home. As with anything, there is some excellent information out there, but also there is such a thing as "too much information." There are a couple different "schools" of Feng Shui, and it can get really complex. Therefore, to simplify your internet browsing, just type in "Feng Shui nursery" and see what comes up.

If anything, at least find out your child's personal element and "Kua" number to arrange their furniture and crib so their head faces the best direction. Instructions and charts are available on About.com in which you can easily discover this information. In Feng Shui, bed placement is extremely important, because it is the sole piece of furniture most intimately connected to your personal energy.

My son had been continually waking up in the middle of the night for the past several months, and one of the things we did that helped was to change his room around so that the headboard of his bed is facing the opposite direction, since he always preferred to sleep that way, anyhow. Since we did that, he seems to be sleeping through the night much more often than not.

Overall in Feng Shui, the most helpful tips are to make sure there is minimal clutter, easy accessibility to the items you need, plenty of open space, and the proper use of color to evoke a desired state (such as sleep!).

Capture Moments

DOCUMENT EVERYTHING! HANDPRINTS, FOOTPRINTS, videos, pictures, anything you can, because it goes by fast as lightening. Even if you can't scrapbook or don't have time (who does?) you can do it digitally by creating a digital scrapbook on sites such as Snapfish or Shutterfly.

My ex-boss had a brilliant idea of creating a calendar of her daughter's special moments each month from the previous year for the coming year every December. For babies, you can get a 13-month milestone calendar from Hallmark that has stickers of each milestone such as "First Fruit," "Crawls," and "Says Mama." I highly recommend this milestone calendar. I've done it for both my babies and it has been amazing to be able to look back and see their progress and the things I had written about what they did and when.

Also (this takes some time, but I did this when they were sleeping), I got the idea from my sister to do a "monthly e-mail" for the baby's first year to family and close friends. I took (and continue to take) dozens of digital pictures all the time, from both my regular camera and my phone. Then, when they turned another month old, I uploaded them to my Picasa software, went through them, and chose the cutest ones I could find to store in a separate folder I called (for example) "Victoria – 6 Months." Then, I uploaded them to our digital photo album online, and sent the link to everyone in an email. That way, everyone could see the pictures and it didn't take up any memory space as opposed to sending actual picture files which could get quite large.

At the end of my baby's first year, I went through only those monthly folders (or e-mails) and printed about five to eight pictures of the cutest ones and scrapbooked those. This way, at least I didn't have to go through every single photo for the entire year, because that would be too overwhelming. That is what I did for William also – to complete his first year scrapbook – albeit he was almost two when it was completed; but at least I did it! I'm so glad I did, and I know you would be, too, if you can do it. That first year only happens once, and it is amazing to see all their "firsts," milestones, and growth. Of course, it would have been even easier if I had printed a few of my favorite pictures each month, and then I wouldn't have had to go back at all at the end of the year, but I liked that I was able to go back and reminisce, anyway.

I will say, however, that those plaster of Paris handprint and footprint molds are very tough to do! I ruined a couple in the process before I got it right, because it dried too quickly. The non-toxic ink prints are much easier, albeit still tricky with an infant, but totally worth it. There are some kits made of a "foamy" substance that hardens, which work pretty good, although not as exact in detail, but still cute. Anything you do to document this precious time, you will not regret.

Alternative Healing

GIVE ALTERNATIVE HEALING A chance – don't knock it until you try it! When your newborn is in the middle of a 101° fever, our natural reaction as new parents may be fear and panic. We instinctively want them to get better immediately. However, it serves you and your child best to know when to run to the medicine cabinet and when to use more gentle, natural methods to assist Mother Nature in Her own work.

I'm in no way suggesting not giving your child needed medication, but just to stop and ask yourself if it *is* really "needed." For example, my two-year-old son had a slowly-rising fever the day after a local summer festival we attended. His temperature started at 100°, but then rose to 101° a few hours later. We had him take a nap and he wanted his blanket. I hesitated, but let him have it, figuring he'd "burn" the fever out of him. It worked. After his nap, he joyfully ran out of his room and it was back down to 100°, and then back to normal the next morning.

I told myself if it got to 102°, I would give him the Children's Tylenol, but I am glad I held off this time. In the past, I've called his pediatrician, and he said to hold off on the medicine because it was best to let the fever spike so that it "burns out" and goes away faster – i.e., whatever was causing the fever meant that the body is handling what it needed to handle and to leave it alone. Mind you, this advice was from an allopathic doctor!

A fantastic resource for me has been my Holistic Moms Network website (www.holisticmoms.org), under the "Holistic Living" tab, "Resources and Articles" link, "Holistic Health" link. Many of the Moms in my Holistic Moms Network swear by certain vitamins, herbs, oils, and natural tonics, about which they are so extremely knowledgeable. I can never keep it straight, so I just check this site or ask them and learn from the e-mail loop about questions other Moms have.

Another case where alternative methods can help is the dreaded colic. Parents whose infants have colic have found success by taking them to a Chiropractor for regular adjustments. My daughter was born quite quickly and I had an instinct that she had a misalignment because she would cry when I put her down and otherwise cry seemingly for no reason. Although it wasn't for hours at a time, such as with colic, it was enough to raise a red flag for me. At a month old, I took her to my Chiropractor for her first adjustment, and afterward she slept straight away! I would continue to take her after that to make sure all was going well, and to this day she is fine with the adjustments. Most people would hesitate doing that for a newborn, but her immediate relaxation and contentment after the adjustment assured me that my judgment was correct.

Furthermore, I have learned that a child's temperament can be affected by their diet. That caught my attention! I felt I could not go wrong by mashing up some bananas, carrots, yams, and several other things for her so I could be sure she was getting pure food versus processed food with all kinds of preservatives in it, and it was so much easier to make than people think.

Aside from Chiropractors, other fields of holistic care include Acupressure, Acupuncture, Cranio-Sacral Therapy, Homeopathy, Napropathy, and Naturopathy. A good resource to find a holistic practitioner is under http://community.wellnesspossibilities. com/holistic-moms/, www.holisticpractitioner.net or www. holisticassociation.org.

Massage

A HUGE ISSUE WITH many parents (including me!) is getting their child to sleep and/or stay asleep. I learned about infant massage from several articles and not only does it help, but the health benefits from massage in both children and adults are becoming more and more recognized.

In children, massage strengthens the bond between child and parent, helps relieve stress and anxiety, and stimulates both physical and mental development. Studies have shown increased skin-to-skin contact helps premature babies gain weight.

In adults, massage also helps with stress and anxiety, of course, but also promotes better sleeping, digestion, circulation, and even boosts the immune system by increasing the white blood cell count.

Personally, I try and treat myself to a massage as often as I can, which, as of this writing, ends up being about once every six months. However, I was thrilled to discover that my insurance actually paid for a massage in my Chiropractor's office as part of the office visit! Make sure to check your insurance for that one! Unfortunately, I had to switch insurances to an HMO when I became a SAHM, but when I had my PPO, I was able to get a half-hour massage before my adjustment every month, because it counted as part of the treatment since it was within the same office visit! It helped tremendously with my shoulders and upper back from the physical strain of nursing and carrying the diaper bag.

For my children, when they get worked up (such as when my then-two-year-old refuses his bedtime or nap), I try to calm him down by giving him a quick full-body massage starting with his shoulders, neck, arms, back, and legs. Sometimes it tickles him, so I have to be careful not to get him going, but to wind him down. If he's really upset, I'll gently do his temples and the top of his head. He loves the special attention from Mommy and I think it helps him sleep better.

Another way I "sneak" a quick massage in is when I give them their baths. When I wash their hair, I massage their scalp, and try to do the same when washing their arms, hands, legs, feet, and back, and again when I put lotion on them afterward.

To-Do Lists

IT'S BEEN SAID THAT "Cleanliness is next to Godliness." I relate that to cleanliness of mind. If my mind is clear, I can feel closer to Spirit. When my mind is cluttered, feeling peaceful and spiritual is almost impossible for me. That said, I live on making my little daily "to-do" lists and crossing things off of them. Perhaps it also gives me a sense of control amidst the chaos. Either way, it works.

When I check things off of a list, I get a feeling of accomplishment. So, at the end of the day after dinner, I sit down and look at my list and see what I've done and what hasn't been done. I can then choose to keep certain items for the next day's list and re-prioritize. It is important that I put only two or three things maximum to really aim to accomplish so that I don't get too frazzled. There is enough that comes up during the day that I must attend to in the normal care of the children and home, such as diapers, feedings, dishes, etc. These types of things don't make the daily list because it is a given that it always needs to be done.

The way I do it is as follows: After dinner, my husband takes the kids downstairs in the basement to play. I clear off the table, do the dishes, wipe the counters, and then sit at the kitchen table to make my list for the next day. I get a yellow post-it note and write down what I want to accomplish. However, I keep in mind not to stress about accomplishing everything, so I put stars next to only about three "priority" things I really want to get done. I circle the stars of the one(s) I absolutely must get done. I end up with my list of a few things to focus on (in order of priority), then a few "optional" things that I can do when I can or else I try to do them sometime during the rest of week. At the end of the day, I will re-prioritize and re-write for the following day. This way, whether I do everything, the top things, or just the "must-do" thing, I have three levels of accomplishment and I end up happy with getting anything done. I set myself up for winning.

It feels good to get things done and have peace of mind. That feeling makes me calmer and less stressed knowing the important things are being accomplished, such as caring for the children to the best of my ability, which is always the number one priority.

The Ultimate Stress Reducer

To SEE GOD, JUST look into the eyes of your child. When all is said and done and I've come to my wits end with my toddler for fighting me on his nap for the hundredth time, I just stop and stare into his big, beautiful hazel eyes and I am in awe. He knows he has me tied around his little finger and I always will be.

As for my daughter, when she smiles, her entire face lights up just like the sun. She is simply gorgeous and I know I am in deep trouble in about 15 years. No matter how much she fusses from teething or digestion, and I feel so terrible about it, I just look into her darling angel eyes and my heart just melts.

Just try it; I am sure that this trick will work for you as an immediate stress-reducer as well, even if that little one is the very cause of your stress at the moment!

Section Two
With the Kids

THESE ARE SUGGESTIONS OF some fun things I have discovered that I could do with the kids that also connect us with God.

Celebrate the Seasons

I WAS FORTUNATE TO meet a friend who is into nature celebrations and facilitates Equinox and Solstice celebrations at our local Theosophical Society grounds each quarter. It is a fantastic way to get the kids familiar with nature and the idea of connection to Spirit through recognizing and celebrating the changes of the season.

There is a wonderful book called "Celebrating the Great Mother: A Handbook of Earth-Honoring Activities for Parents and Children" by Cait Johnson and Maura D. Shaw, which has activities specifically for kids to do during the Equinoxes and Solstices. For example, to celebrate the Spring Equinox we planted seeds, and to celebrate the Summer Solstice, we made crowns. The celebration ceremonies include a potluck meal, drumming, songs, prayers, and Dances of Universal Peace. The kids really enjoy these activities and celebration ceremonies, so I highly recommend trying this!

Christenings

IN ALMOST EVERY RELIGION or culture, there is some type of welcoming ceremony for the baby into the family. Some parents have Christenings, some have Baptisms and others have Naming Ceremonies. I chose to have Naming Ceremonies for both of my children. These ceremonies are deeply personal and sacred to the parents. Specific customs and traditions vary, depending on the parents' religious/spiritual preference. I find that many parents who did not practice a religion (or have not practiced in a long time) decide to choose one and perform this ceremony for their child, because it allows for some kind of special induction to the family with love.

Of course, the child will not remember this, but you are, in a sense, setting him or her up with a spiritual support system. You are providing your child with a resource in the Ministers or Priests who perform this ceremony, along with their affiliated church community, any Godmothers or Godfathers the child may have, and all the friends and family who gather there.

However, an added benefit ends up being that the parents now have this support system for themselves as well! Something to keep in mind as time goes by, life happens, and you need an extra shoulder to lean on.

Church

WE HESITATE TO THINK of taking little ones to church because of their high energy. Yet, most churches do have a "cry room," and perhaps even a facilitator for the younger age group. I, myself, had the opportunity to be that facilitator for my church and we named it the "Small Wonders" program, after the name of the "cry room" it was held in.

Although the children are too young to really understand the lessons, I created a modified program for them including singing the church service songs with them and reading them inspirational children's books and lessons (see Resources).

It is nice to have the children be exposed to a spiritual community at a young age, so that they have that foundation when they need it later in life. By then, they'll have a whole other group of adults and ministers to talk to when they don't want to talk to Mom and Dad.

If you have always gone to church, continue going. Community is a great thing to have at this important juncture of your life, and healthy for the child(ren) as well. Granted, it is a lot of work to get the kids dressed and out the door, but it has its advantages. One is that it is good for you to do as many of the same things you did before baby/kids. Another advantage is that it fosters the child's sense of a spiritual community in which you would be nurturing him/her as they grow, so it's best to get them used to it now.

However, it is a good idea to have Daddy or someone watch the baby/kids and go to church yourself once in a while, or else see if you can have a fellow Mom watch them there. Many churches have a facilitator for this age group, such as my church, www.

dupagecenter.org. This way, you can direct your full attention to the service and really get the most out of it without having to also keep an eye on the kids. I believe in the idea of going with them, but obviously it is not the same as when you get to go alone. Plus, it is a way to get some much-needed spiritual replenishment during this time in your life when you really need it.

Praying and having a spiritual practice is a fantastic thing to have and be able to lean on when you are at your wits' end with your crying baby or whining toddler. From it, you are better able to feel love and gratitude for the fun times when you are joyfully tickling them and laughing with them. God gets you through both the good and the bad – God gets you through it all.

Dances of Universal Peace

I DISCOVERED THESE DANCES from the same friend who introduced me to the seasonal celebrations, because she took her daughter. She taught me that I could easily take my baby to these dances by holding her in a front-baby carrier. It's great exercise, too! So, I took both children by holding my daughter in the carrier and having my son dancing with us.

I would describe these dances as "prayers in motion," so although fun for the kids, it needs to have a certain amount of respect as well, just like church. My toddler really did enjoy the dances for the first hour, and got better at keeping up as I continued to take him, but after a while, he'd want to go home after the break.

Furthermore, after my daughter outgrew the carrier and my son became restless, it was no longer respectful to take them to the adult group, because they broke the circle often and ran around on their own, which was understandably too distracting for the other participants.

Fortunately, my friend is studying to be a facilitator herself, so she is creating a Dances class especially for kids. That way, we will be able to bring our kids and continue to teach them the prayers and steps. Then, if (when) they break free and run around, it would be okay, because it would be a class solely for kids, which is a different energy and purpose than the one for adults.

Visit www.dancesofuniversalpeace.org for more information.

Drumming Circles

I NEVER WOULD HAVE considered bringing my children to a drumming circle if it had not been for a wonderful lady I met in my church congregation named Darlene Palese (www. awithheartinhandpetcare.com). She loves kids and insisted I bring mine. I am so glad I did! My son loved the drumming and he even got into the rhythm by running around the outside of the circle, which (fortunately!) the participants did not mind.

Of course, this would not work with all groups, so be sure to check with the group leader before you attempt this. Unfortunately, there is a small "window" of time between the baby and toddler ages where this will work. In months after, when he was nearing four, he seemed to get bored of it and didn't want to do it anymore. Yet, my one-year-old still enjoyed it and would pick up some instruments to participate. Perhaps she'll continue to want to go. However, one time when my son saw us going without him, he changed his mind and wanted to go again as well. It's hit-or-miss, sometimes, with toddlers.

I love the idea of getting the kids to experience the feeling of group drumming – the intensity of it, the sound of the different drums and other instruments harmonizing, and being able to participate. If anything, it's a foundation for them to accompany me in the future and to learn about other cultures that do this. I encourage them to play their instruments at home for their own enjoyment, so they can learn about music and hopefully foster their love of it. In addition, it's very therapeutic to get all your frustrations out in the drumming, if needed.

Expose Them to Other Cultures

I HAD THE PLEASURE of "receiving Amma's embrace" with my children and my Mother this summer. Amma is considered an Indian "Hugging Saint" who blesses you with a loving hug. See www.amma.org for a full biography and program description.

What was particularly special about this experience was that I got a chance to introduce my children to the Indian culture in an interactive, joyful way. The experience took a long time (about three hours), so it's certainly not feasible for all children, but you just never know until you try. I simply take my kids everywhere and give it a shot. I was glad I did this one.

It was a delight for the senses! We entered the building and saw hundreds of people dressed in traditional, colorful Indian clothing. We could hear lovely, soft meditation music playing. The smell of delicate, sweet scent incense was burning. There were several Indian and American cuisine vendors set up for lunch with delicious food. They had their first taste of authentic Indian delicacies at the ages of three and one year old!

Obviously, the point of all this is to teach my children that people come in all shapes, sizes, and colors, so that they won't be the kid in school who makes fun of someone for being different or "weird." Ideally, I would think that early exposure to other cultures will pave the way for them to grow into tolerant, open-minded adults, which I believe this world sorely needs more of, and I am hopeful that our generation of children will be the ones to become just that.

Get a Pet

IT'S ALL ABOUT THE timing on this one. If you don't already have a pet, I would not advise doing this anywhere near the time baby is due (as I did – big mistake!). A good time would be about six months before the baby's arrival, to make sure the pet is compatible with your home and personality; or else at least six months to a year after the baby is born, so that you are well-adjusted to the baby first.

On the other hand, it is another responsibility added on during a time when you completely have your hands full. So, if you aren't an "animal lover" or if your pet adds more stress, then do yourself and your family a big favor and skip this chapter.

However, with the right animal(s), they are very relaxing to pet and play with. Added bonus: If you have a trained dog or cat, it sure is nice to have something *obey* you for a change!

Aside from helping to relieve stress, another bonus to having a pet is that it teaches your child to love and care for animals, as they also are part of God's creation, and should be treated with kindness and respect. Children who learn to treat animals well are learning compassion and responsibility. As it is always said, example is the best teacher.

If allergies prevent this from being an option for you, then you can take your child on "field trips" to the local pet store or to the zoo, in which case, they are still learning love and respect for animals. Education about animals breeds understanding, which breeds compassion, which is another trait sorely needed in this world. What better way to improve society than to raise compassionate children? Animals can help.

Holidays

I LOVE THE HOLIDAYS! The word "holiday" originated from the words "holy day," so most people think of "the holidays" as being Christmas, Hanukkah, and Kwanzaa. To me, "the holidays" always began with Halloween, and included Thanksgiving, Christmas and New Year's. However, it turned out that both my children were born in the fall, so now for me, "the holidays" include their birthdays as well.

Regardless of which "winter break" holidays you celebrate, if any, there is no question that this is a very special time of year for many people. Somehow, with the nights being longer and the weather getting cooler, it is natural for us to turn "inward," both in body and mind. We snuggle up in warm blankets, cuddle by fires, and become more reflective and sentimental during this time.

Most of all, it is a magical time for children. Being parents, we get to witness firsthand the joy of dressing them up at Halloween, teaching them gratitude at Thanksgiving, and surprising them with presents at Christmas/Hanukkah/Kwanzaa. Holidays bring out the child in us, too, and celebrating them to the best of your ability is most certainly one of the most effective and fulfilling ways to connect to spirit – through joy, laughter, and love.

Labyrinths

A LABYRINTH IS A winding path generally in the shape of a circle which takes you to a center point from which you follow it back to the start. Many people use labyrinths for solving problems, gaining clarity, promoting relaxation, and developing intuition. They can be found at retreat centers, parks, churches, and even some hospitals. You can also use a wooden finger board or paper pattern. I prefer walking the path outdoors, because it has a powerful healing and calming effect.

I generally use labyrinths as a personal "clarification" tool. However, I discovered they can be good for kids as well. I came across a children's wooden lap-sized "double finger" labyrinth under the "Labyrinth Resources" / "Labyrinth Kid's Corner" link in the www.relax4life.com website. It is said to help stimulate and balance both the right and left sides of the brain together, leading to greater mental focus and physical relaxation. As the child plays with it using both hands, both sides of the brain begin to work in harmony which relaxes the child and helps with creativity. It also says "there is also good indication that working with this pattern may assist functioning in conditions such as ADD, ADHD, Dyslexia, Developmental Delays etc." Interestingly, it also states that if two children play with it together, it is supposed to enhance their intuitive connection.

Before purchasing a wooden labyrinth, however, what I've done instead is downloaded the blank pages from that site and taped them together to construct a paper double-sided labyrinth. I showed my son how to do it, and let both children color it (both single and double-sided). That way, they are exposed to what it is and can play with it however they like, for now, until they get older and I can show them the traditional way. Regarding the life-sized outdoor labyrinths, my kids also like running around and across the loops versus following the path, and that's great fun for them, too. Of course, I would only let them do that when no one else is using it!

Personally, I have always enjoyed visiting and walking my local labyrinth before embarking on any major life endeavor (weather permitting, since it is outdoors). I like to center myself and pray while doing this. You'll have to have someone watch the baby(ies) or if possible, do it while pregnant. There is one at the Theosophical Society in Wheaton, Illinois and also at the Garfield Park Conservatory in Chicago, Illinois.

When I was pregnant with my second child and before I began my time as being a SAHM, I went to the labyrinth on a beautiful June morning. Going in, I didn't really have an idea of what I expected to get out of it, but I knew I had to go.

As I stepped on the first stone circle, I just cleared my head and began on the path, thinking about my life up until now. When I got to the center, I gave thanks for all my blessings and all the blessings yet to come. I thought about all the things coming in the near future and visions about what I wanted things to be like. All of a sudden, I got the idea for this book. After exiting the labyrinth, I just sat on a bench for a while reflecting and left feeling refreshed and clear-headed.

In hindsight, perhaps that was what I pretty much expected all along (clarity). What I did not expect was to leave there with the task of writing a whole new book! However, that is what happens sometimes when you make contact with the Spirit – you get what you need, not what you ask for or "think" you need.

Spiritual Children's Books

I WAS SO PLEASED to discover that my favorite spiritual authors also wrote books for children! It is important to me to pass along my New Thought beliefs which portray a benevolent, positive, and all-inclusive God whom I learned about through many of these wonderful authors. I am thrilled to share with you that they have adapted their messages for the little ones.

Louise Hay, Wayne Dyer, Deepak Chopra, Byron Katie, Doreen Virtue, and others have several children's books available at www.hayhouse.com. I particularly enjoy reading my children Louise Hay's *I Think I Am* about the power of affirmations.

Neale Donald Walsch has written *The Little Soul and the Sun, The Little Soul and the Earth*, and *Santa's God*. His message is to teach children about their inherent value and connection to God. The books can be found at www.conversationswithgod.org.

Another source is the book club OneSpirit, www.onespirit.com. Under "Children's Fiction" you will find inspirational books such as *One Love* and *Every Little Thing* based on the songs by Bob Marley, written by his daughter Cedella Marley. However, since this is a book club, the titles change regularly.

Fortunately, I have also been privy to some good books for young kids on new thought teachings, being a facilitator in my church for the 0-4 age group. I was given *10 Big Ideas of New Thought Teaching for Kids 3-8* by Reverend Nancy Zala, which has simple lessons and coloring pages. There is also an upcoming series of four books titled, *How to Remember Who You Are* available at www.howtorememberwhoyouare.com. The characters are four animated puppies named Dusty, Snuggles, Bouncer, and Spot who each have a different lesson to teach with lesson plans, coloring pages, activities, and a song. The first book is available to download as a free trial.

More inspirational books on affirmations and new thought concepts for children can be found through the publisher DeVorss & Company at www.devorss.com.

Spiritual Children's Movies

THANKS TO FILM PRODUCER, Stephen Simon, there is a new genre of movies titled "Spiritual Cinema." He coined the term for inspirational films that leave you with a good feeling inside that aren't filled with violence, nudity, and foul language. He co-founded a movie club called "The Spiritual Cinema Circle," which sends you a volume of films each month that you get to keep. The volumes typically consist of three shorts and one feature-length film, followed by film discussions with Steven, one of the directors, and a guest member. My husband and I are charter members and have been very pleased with the selections. I have shared them with family and friends who also enjoyed them. I encourage you to visit this wonderful site for more information at www.spiritualcinemacircle.com.

The club themes are mainly tailored to adults, but several of the films are family-friendly. He even created a compilation for kids titled "Kids Cinema Circle." Although my son was only two, he enjoyed watching some of a movie titled "Make Believe" which is about teen magicians. He was enthralled by their card, coin, and ring tricks. I was inspired by the teens' talent and passion, and that they were involved in something that motivated them and was enjoyable and entertaining. That is the point of this genre – for the movies to inspire you.

The ones that are ideal for kids are their animated short films ("shorts") they have from time-to-time. Subjects range from meditating monks to techno-obsessed family members. It so happened my Mother-in-Law passed away this past August when William was just 3½ and Victoria was 1½. Victoria is too young to understand, but for William, my husband and I felt we needed to explain to him why he wouldn't see Grandma at family gatherings anymore. Coincidentally, that month's volume of Spiritual Cinema Circle contained two animated shorts – one of which was titled "The Fabulous Flying Books of Mr. Morris Lessmore" about life and death. It was a blessing to be able to use the film as a gentle way to discuss the situation with William in concepts I knew he could understand that weren't too scary for him.

There are many mainstream Hollywood films that are inspiring for children, but unfortunately you have to often pick through all the "cartoon violence" and "mild language" that I would prefer not to have my child exposed to, particularly at such a young age. I dislike having to explain to my son why he can't actually do the things he sees on screen, and I don't want him to be desensitized to violence. At least with the Spiritual Cinema Circle, Stephen lets you know upfront if a film is appropriate for the entire family or only the adults, and I have been very pleased with the selections. These are rare, often independent, films I would never know about if it weren't for this club; as a parent, I fully support it.

Another good resource is Netflix. I was thrilled to discover that they actually have a section titled "Faith and Spirituality for Kids"! My favorite is "The Littlest Angel" because of the moral of the story...I won't give it away, though, you'll have to see it for yourself.

Yoga for Toddlers

As MOST OF US are aware, the health benefits of yoga are far-ranging, including body awareness, relaxation, exercise, and centering. However, I never considered Yoga for toddlers until we had a presenter at one of my monthly Holistic Mom's Network meetings who did a session with us and the kids. It was a big hit!

There are specific Yoga classes designed especially for young children. I took my 2½ year-old son to "Yoga Camp" for a week. Each class was 1½ hours for one week, Monday through Friday, and it was a drop-off class, so I was able to spend time alone with my 7-month-old daughter. My son really enjoyed the class. I got a list of the poses so I could practice doing them with him at home. I decided to incorporate some of the poses into his bedtime routine to help him wind down. Eventually, he created his own "poses" and we have a lot of fun with them!

If you look up "Yoga for toddlers" online, you will find a multitude of resources. However, unless you are skilled in Yoga yourself, I would not recommend doing the poses with your toddler unless you take him or her to a class taught by a professional, just to be safe. It is best to make sure you are doing the poses correctly to prevent any type of injury or strain. Once mastered, however, it is great fun for your child and offers many benefits, such as teaching body awareness, managing stress, increasing focus, and sharpening concentration skills. I am always open to anything that enhances my child's physical and mental well-being, and this was a great discovery I share with other parents.

Section Three
Just for Mom

These suggestions are offered in the spirit that they could help you to center and balance yourself in order to be the best Mom you can be!

Affirmations

AFFIRMATIONS ARE POSITIVE ONE-LINE statements you repeat to yourself over and over. This is slightly different from simply using positive self-talk, because these are short, present-tense phrases used to evoke a feeling of conviction in the moment. It is "reprogramming" your brain to think differently, but also to use the power of emotion to manifest your chosen desire.

I created my own affirmation cards by first writing a list of healing statements. I carried this list with me to read to myself over and over for several days, modifying anything that didn't sound or feel right until it was. It is important to use only positive words, rather than "not," "no," "won't," and the like. For example, instead of saying "I will not lose my temper with the children" you can say, "I will practice patience and speak to my children in a calm, gentle tone." See the Appendix for some affirmations just for parents.

A friend of mine shared an excellent idea with me on how she does her affirmations: she keeps them in list form (versus cards) and reads them while she's blow drying her hair and/or brushing her teeth. This is an ideal time because you're either doing those activities in the morning before you start your day or at night before bed. In fact, doing them at both times would be highly effective.

Whenever or however you choose to do them, the main focus is the feeling behind them. If you just read through them without conceptualizing them, it most likely won't do you any good, unless perhaps pure repetition is what works for you. However, most people find that truly focusing on the words and feelings 100% brings about true and lasting results.

There are so many resources for affirmations. It is good to discover many to find the ones that resonate best with you. Ultimately, however, the most effective exercise would be for you to create your own. That way, they will be especially meaningful and powerful for you.

Breaks

As WITH THE MEDITATION, you might be saying, "Breaks? What breaks? No such thing!" True, but for your own sanity, you truly need to figure out a method to get some time to yourself. Not only do you need your "Me Time" to breathe, but also to do something you enjoy that is your own and separate from the kids.

If you have one child, you get at least some respite when they nap. However, if you have more than one and their naps are on different schedules or one of them no longer naps (as in my case!), it can be extremely tough. In that case, enlist an army of people to alternate times to help you schedule at least one weekly break (if not more!). Ideas are: Daddy, Grandma, Auntie, Sitter, Day Care, Friend, or Neighbor. Ideally, someone who you don't have to pay is great, so if you can't get Daddy, Mom, or Sister, then try to switch babysitting with a friend or neighbor so that you both can benefit. I did that with my dear neighbor across the street during the summer when her kids were out of school, which she cleverly titled, "Kid Swap" days!

Without breaks, you will burn out and become something you aren't. You may find yourself short-tempered, over-sensitive, and isolated. Your mind may become overrun with negative thoughts, because you will end up resenting the fact that you "lost yourself." Don't do that to yourself or your family. Try scheduling a weekly break for one month to see how it goes and work from there.

Mind you, going grocery shopping alone does NOT count! Do something to recharge your soul. Read in silence at your local library. Take a one-night art class through the park district. Do some journaling over a delicious cup of tea at a local café. Have dinner with a friend. Visit a salt cave. Walk a labyrinth. Attend a spiritual circle of some kind (intention circle, blessing circle, drumming circle, etc. – see Resources). This is something just for you, to replenish your creativity, relax, vent, or simply pause. This is time worthwhile.

Body Awareness

IN THE WHIRLWIND THAT is now your life with a baby and/or toddler, your focus is all about them and you easily forget about yourself. After my six-week post-partum checkup and when I felt ready, I got to focusing on my own body regarding exercise and awareness.

What I mean by "body awareness" is different than just exercising. I am referring to being more conscious of how I hold and position my body in daily activity, such as walking, sitting, and lifting.

For instance, I found it helpful to purposely hold my core muscles in while lifting anything, such as the baby in the car seat, the groceries, or my toddler. Another practice you hear about constantly is doing your Kegels. So, I would do my best to remember to do them anytime I was sitting for a length of time.

Because I stopped thinking about it, I found myself having terrible posture since I was nursing and bending down to play with the kids. Every now and then while I was sitting on a park bench or at home on the floor, I became aware that I was slouching, and needed to remind myself to sit up straight and to walk tall like I used to.

After practicing body awareness for a while, it will become a habit, just like anything, and it will be second-nature. The healthier you are, the better you will feel and be able to enjoy this special, fleeting time with your baby(ies) all the more. Getting started is the key!

Breathing Exercises

BEING ABLE TO STOP and do a quick breathing exercise has been extremely helpful. It only takes a minute or two (however long you are able), and you can do them anywhere. I've done them waiting with the kids in the pediatrician's office and even having lunch at the park with them. I learned the following exercises from Dr. Andrew Weil, as outlined on pages 204-207 in his book *Spontaneous Healing*.

The first, most basic breathing exercise is just to observe your breath. This involves simply sitting and noticing your inhalations and exhalations without trying to force anything either way.

The second exercise is to "start" with exhaling versus thinking about the inhalation being the beginning of the breathing cycle. By starting with the exhalation, you are focusing on releasing all the breath out of your lungs so as to take in a fuller breath.

The third exercise is to "let yourself be breathed," but this one cannot be done in public because you have to lie down. While in a flat position on the floor, you visualize the universe "breathing" you and it is very relaxing.

The fourth exercise is a stimulating breath, also called "bellows breath." This is an excellent one to get you going in the morning and only takes a few seconds. In fact, I had to use this while driving a couple of times, because I was so tired. I was afraid I would fall asleep at the wheel, and I don't drink caffeine, so I needed something else to wake me up right in the moment, and this did the trick. However, I would most definitely practice this at home until you make sure you get the cadence, so you don't hyperventilate. I've done this several times, so I knew I was safe.

While keeping your mouth closed, you rapidly inhale and exhale through your nose very quickly and you hear the air going in and out. It should only be done for about 5-10 seconds. Then, see how you feel, and only do it once or twice more, maximum, if you still need to.

The fifth and final breathing exercise Dr. Weil recommends is called the "relaxing breath," and this is the one I use the most. You exhale as much as you can out of your mouth with a quiet "whooshing" sound, close your mouth, then inhale deeply through your nose counting to four inside your mind. Then, hold for a count of seven and exhale again to the count of eight. The cycle is inhale four, hold seven, and exhale eight. He recommends doing the entire cycle four times, then return to normal breathing.

I highly recommend checking out Dr. Weil's book for the full description before attempting any of these.

Emotional Freedom Technique (EFT)

I FIRST LEARNED ABOUT EFT at a workshop at my church. I liked it right away because it was easy and quick. It was something I could do in less than five minutes, and the results were real and lasting. I also appreciated the fact that I could do this by myself on myself in the privacy of my own home and on my own schedule, because having to schedule a session with a practitioner was more inconvenient for me at this point in my life since I'd have to get a sitter. Ultimately, however, I was looking for quick, easy things I could do to calm down and center myself while I was with the kids during the day, so this was right up my alley. The fact that it is also free is another huge bonus!

In a nutshell, you identify an emotional or physical problem you are having, and then say it out loud while performing a series of tapping specific points on your body to clear away negative energy in your meridians. Meridians are energy pathways which are used in Traditional Chinese Medicine (TCM) techniques such as acupuncture and acupressure.

The basic outline of the process goes like this: First, you continually strike the outer sides of your hands together (such as using a "karate chop" movement on them) while saying the phrase out loud or in your mind "Although I have *(this problem)*, I deeply love and respect myself." Then, you repeat the problem out loud or in your mind (such as "Headache") and start with tapping the inside point of your eyebrows (while stating the problem), then the temple points on the sides of your eyes, then the bone underneath your eyes, then your upper lip below your nose, then the bottom lip just above the chin, then your collarbone area at the top of your chest just inside your shoulder blades, then underneath your arms at the sides of your ribcage, then the bottom portion of your ribs, then finishing the tapping series at the top of your head, all the while repeating the problem out loud or in your mind. You check in with yourself after and see how you feel and if you need to repeat the process. I highly recommend you do a You Tube search to find a video so you can see this in action to identify the points correctly. Also, you could do an internet search to find a diagram outlining the points and steps of the process as well.

An example of how it worked for me was one morning when I woke up with a slight headache that progressively got worse as the day went on. I didn't have a chance to tend to it until after the kids were asleep (I don't take aspirin), but I knew I wouldn't be able to sleep if I didn't do something, so I performed the EFT series on myself. It worked! I was so relieved.

You can use EFT for anything from pain in specific parts of your body (such as a headache) to more intense problems, such as anxiety, post-partum depression or clearing away emotional trauma, just to name a few. Sometimes you may find you need to do it a few times on the same issue to ensure the "charge" is cleared away. Other times you may find other "sub-issues" come up that were buried inside which rise to the surface as you deal with one issue at a time. It is best to do EFT on any and all issues that come up. The sense of lightness and clearing I felt was wonderful. For me, getting rid of negative emotional garbage makes me better able to be a more attentive, loving parent, because then I don't have any baggage dragging me down.

Distance Healing

ONE OF THE BEST resources I've found for spiritual connection has been the concept of distance work. I was first introduced to this by Deb Hanneman who does remote energy healings. Her site is www.zen-mommies.com.

I had my first Energy Healing Session with her on Monday, October, 17, 2011. Before then, I had been feeling like I had been having some trouble taking deep breaths and some tension issues in certain parts of my body. In the days that followed the session, I did much better in both areas.

At first, I did not know what to expect, because I had never done a remote session before. However, it was the strangest thing because when she began, I literally felt an almost instant "lightness" and very delicate "tingling" below my ribcage, in my diaphragm, and chest. I actually felt "lighter" as the healing was happening, and in the moments after. The heaviness never came back, but rather, I had gotten used to the new feeling of lightness.

In our discussion afterward, the things she told me she saw in my aura were dead on target with some personal issues I was having at the time. That also helped tremendously, because it helped me clarify my next steps and gave me something I could work with to prevent too much tension buildup in the future.

I think everyone should try a healing session, because it worked and it was so convenient! Having a toddler and an infant, I just had my Mom come watch them downstairs while I was on the phone. It only took 30 minutes and the effects lasted. In the days after, I still felt lighter than I did before. The tension and pain I had in certain areas of my body had not returned, so I'm pretty happy with it and I highly recommend it!

Another resource for remote work is my friends at "Gang of Girls" productions, Auriel Grace and Donna Damato. They do energy healing sessions and readings over the phone or via Skype. Their websites are www.agangofgirls.com and www.elevateddelights. com.

Formulate Your Mommy Group

CREATE FOR YOURSELF A "Mommy Network" of nonjudgmental, open-hearted women who understand your position. Let them help you if they can, even if it is simply to vent (and sometimes venting is not so simple!). No one truly understands your position unless they have been in it themselves.

Even well-meaning people can make you feel worse – unwillingly, of course. That is why you need a friend or two (or three) "in the trenches with you" (or who has been there!) to rely on through the worst days – when you need reassurance and encouragement, and the best days – when you need to share your enthusiasm for accomplishing even the littlest of things without the judgment of comparison.

Some ideas on where to start are at church, online, or in your neighborhood. You can do a combination of these through Meetup.com where you can find local Mom groups online. I love this site because you can specify your interests as "Spirituality" "Meditation" "Drumming" "Holistic Living" and several others to find like-minded souls near you! Another way to meet Moms is to go to the local library for story time and talk to the Moms there. Also, if you can, sign your child up for a short four- or five-week class where you can meet other Moms.

I discovered the Holistic Mom's Network at a local green fair one year (www.holisticmoms.org). Joining this group was the one of the best things I did for myself and my family. These are a group of like-minded women who are interested in "natural health and mindful parenting" (as quoted from their Welcome page). It was a great help to find other Moms who were interested in the same things I was as a parent. Theirs is an excellent site for like-minded Moms, including green housekeeping tips, organic recipes, and mindful living information. Coincidentally, it just so happens that some of them even hold my similar spiritual beliefs as well. I suppose mindfulness and spirituality go hand-in-hand. It was important to me to include other Moms in my "Mommy Network" that were also interested in spirituality, so it was a nice bonus to find some here in this group as well! I met my friend who does the seasonal celebrations and Dances of Universal Peace via this group! Visit www.holisticmoms.org to find a chapter near you.

Keep in mind the group you start out with may not be the group you end up with, but it is good to start somewhere.

Friends

FRIENDS ARE MUCH HARDER to have time for when you are a new Mom. However, ironically, this is the time when you need them the most. You're all caught up in the newness of being a Mommy and the wonder and blessing of your children, but at the same time, it is so emotionally and physically taxing on the mind and body that you need real help. Your husband can only do what he can, but he is right there in the trenches with you, so you need to "call on your reserves," so to speak!

It is great to have "working" friends and "going out" friends. You probably have or will soon have other "Mom" friends, but I'm talking here about the girlfriends that you can go out with and talk about anything other than the kids. Of course, you will talk about your kids at some point, because you love them and they are a part of your life now, but I mean that there is a point where you need to get a mental break from it, and here is where your girlfriends are so important.

With "work" friends, you can talk about the "adult" stuff of work and work relationships. If you don't have a paying job at the moment, then these are perhaps people you can talk to at your church or in your neighborhood about relevant group issues, or even ex-co-workers with whom you are still friends with, for example.

With "going out" friends, these are your old high school girlfriends or perhaps friends you used to work with or know from family ties.

At this time in my life, I am blessed to have gotten together with all my old girlfriends from high school through Facebook for our

20-year reunion. In fact, thanks to Facebook, my "reunion" was a year-long event, beginning with having lunch with one of my dearest friends I haven't seen since high school, then graduating to having lunches and dinners with other long-lost high school friends, then monthly get-togethers, a family barbeque with our kids, then finally the official class reunion. To this day, we are blessed to continue the monthly get-togethers and playdates, including our spouses, too!

It has been such an incredible blessing to have found these ladies, who I am so happy have turned out to be just as incredible now as they were back then. It has been a Godsend for me, just when I needed help the most, becoming a Mom of two under three years old.

I didn't know how badly I needed my friends until that first meeting – I felt like I came back to life! Each friend I reconnected with via dinner or lunch date gave a part of myself back to me. It is priceless, and something nearly impossible for me to do on my own, since I was that far gone and I didn't even know it. Those first meetings with them "woke up" something inside of me that I felt I lost. They remembered me as I was and accepted me no matter what I had gone through in my life since then. I didn't know how much I needed that perspective, that reminder, to get me out of the rut I was in at the time. Although I love my children deeply, I had a hard time transitioning from working to being a Stay-At-Home-Mom, and then a few short months after that, transitioning again from being a parent of one to a parent of two. My dear friends could not have come back into my life at a better time.

That said, I have learned it is important to keep your true friends and family close; anyone who you love. If you've lost touch with old friends, make it a point to find them. If you've had a falling out over something trivial, reconcile. You won't even realize how much you've missed them and needed them until you find your way back to them.

We all know that time is scarce when you have little ones, but time with your friends will leave you refreshed and renewed and coming back to your Mom life with a better sense of self, which is so easy to lose in the midst of changing diapers, nursing, and chasing your toddler.

My message in this chapter is this: keep your friends close, make time for them, and create reunions in your life with anyone who was important to you that you let slip away. Do yourself a favor – if you've lost them, go get those girlfriends back!

Go With the Flow

I learned this one the hard way. An example is when I was constantly fighting with my son about his naps. I did some research on Facebook, browsing the parenting pages, and discovered a solution on the Natural Parenting page. A few Moms said they just let their toddler have some quiet time playing and put them to bed early, say 6:00 or 6:30 p.m. No need to fight for a schedule. If s/he naps at 2:30 (versus 1:00) for a couple hours and goes down for the night at 9:30, and you're fine with that, then go with it! This way, you get your quiet time during the day and you can count your blessings! On the other hand, if s/he doesn't want to nap and goes to bed earlier, then that is a bonus, too! Some Moms preferred this because they got more of an evening with their husbands or for themselves versus during the day.

Another example of going with the flow is regarding mealtimes. In speaking with my pediatrician and doing my own research, I learned that toddlers don't normally eat three square meals. I knew about the "snacking throughout the day" tendency from the day care days, but I didn't consider making their meals a bit smaller as well and just make up for it as a "snack" between meals of something healthy such as yogurt, fruit, granola, veggies with dip, and the like. I was constantly struggling with my son to "just eat one more bite." Now, if he's done, I respect that, and I am able to save it as a "snack" for later. I would observe what he ate and just give him a smaller portion so I wouldn't waste food. No more conflict over food.

The message here is to pick your battles, but work with your child to find a happy solution that satisfies both parties, so that you are not needlessly stressing over something easily resolvable.

Have a Hobby

HOBBIES ARE TERRIFIC STRESS relievers. It seems to work best if it is something that is completely your own that you perform alone – without the kids – as part of your "me" time. It should be something that puts you "in the zone" where your mind is in its own place, uninterrupted by anything else.

My favorite hobby at the moment is my writing, but I also enjoy reading inspirational works. It is fun to have a hobby that is creative, so that you can say, "Hey, look what I can do!" just like your kids do when they make a cute art project in class. When I was home with just my son and pregnant with my daughter, I was blessed to be able to finish a latch-hook pillow at night after he went to bed. I started it when I was 12 years old when I had chicken pox and never got back to finishing it off in "pillow" form; I just had the latch-hook part all these years. What an amazing feeling to have completed something over 25 years in waiting! My son's and daughter's first-year scrapbooks were fulfilling accomplishments, too.

I share this with you because if you can somehow try doing something that has meaning to you using any time you can find, it really does help. It puts things in perspective and you can come back to your family refreshed and renewed versus exhausted and spent. Sometimes just one hour spent in renewal of the spirit can outweigh one hour of sleep (*sometimes!*).

Inspirational Reading

I FIND INSPIRATIONAL READING a must to help train my brain to focus on positive, uplifting thoughts. However, I could not always find time to sit down and just read – that was a luxury. Therefore, I had to get creative on this front as well.

Although feeding time is bonding time, after a while I discovered I could also use this time to read. I put a laptop on a table next to me and was able to read e-books and newsletters on it. When reading books and magazines, I could position myself to turn the page with the free hand.

At night, at the very least, I made sure to simply read an inspirational passage before bed. The "Daily Guides" from my Science of Mind magazine worked well for this. It also helped me to have some kind of nightly routine that signaled it was bedtime, even if I was getting up in another couple of hours.

If anything, you always have to go to the bathroom, so keep a self-help or inspirational book in the bathroom to read just a page or two while nature calls. I have read many books this way – sometimes it's the only time I get!

Journal

THIS ONE CAN BE very tough, but it was essential to me. I had to really be creative on this one, because to actually set aside time to journal was out of the question most days. Some tricks I did are as follows.

If I had an idea, I would type it into my phone, which I kept with me at all times for checking the weather, e-mail, Facebook, and most importantly for security reasons (to make sure I could reach someone at a moment's notice). I am blessed to have a phone with an application that I could type notes into. I dated it, so I could track my progress and, if needed, to copy it into my "real" (handwritten) journal notebook at a later date.

At one point, I found that I was using Facebook as my journal. Of course, not for anything too private, but for funny thoughts or anecdotes I wanted to share. I didn't intend to make Facebook my journal, but it was convenient, because I could do it from my phone anywhere anytime. If I wanted to save these posts, I could just go back at a later date to copy and paste them into a Word document or handwrite them into one of my other journals. Fortunately, Facebook saves posts for a pretty long time – I was able to retrieve a post from six months prior, just before my daughter was born!

I also kept a notepad in the pocket of the diaper bag. This way, I would just jot down anything that came to mind. Examples are some random thoughts, things to put on the grocery list, errands I needed to run – whatever came to mind that I knew I needed to write down, otherwise I would forget.

These ideas are not the typical definition of journaling, but you learn to adjust your concept of how you need to achieve your goals when you become a new Mom. If and when I needed to "really" journal, I did it when the kids were sleeping, if I wasn't too exhausted myself. Eventually I got to the point where I could stay up through their naps and do it. I would begin by journaling about what an achievement it was to be able to stay awake through their naps!

If and when there was a time they both napped, I'd be sure to start journaling right away to get the most time out of it before one of them woke up. I'd journal what I felt I needed to and then try to nap myself, even if it was for only ten minutes, which actually did happen once, but at least I was able to journal and then rest for just a bit.

Making this time for yourself is essential because it is like "talking to your Higher Self." You can gain clarity, vent, or just organize your thoughts in the midst of the chaos. It is like your own personal "conversation with God."

Meditate

RIGHT ABOUT NOW, YOU'RE thinking "yeah, right!" All I wanted to do is sleep when the baby slept, but then I never got a chance to "get my head straight" and center myself. When I slept every chance I could, everything just became a blur, which is what happens in the beginning. A month or two after the birth of your child, however, you will begin to recuperate, and rebuilding (or building) a meditation practice will work wonders for you in terms of putting things in perspective and getting you centered for the most important job in your life.

As difficult it is having a newborn, it is possible to sneak some meditation in. Here are a couple of ways.

Do it while baby is sleeping. Obviously, you need to still be somewhat alert for when baby wakes, which is why at times meditating is even better than sleeping, since you're still awake.

Do it while waiting for baby or toddler to sleep. In the middle of the night, my daughter would wake and cry when she was an infant and that is where I first learned to do this. I would put her back to sleep, leave the room, and wait outside her door to listen to see if she would cry again. During this time, I would meditate. Now, I do the same for my preschool son. He is still in the habit of someone being with him in his room while he falls asleep at night, so I just meditate on the rug next to his bed. Bonus is that it teaches him what meditation is as well – by example. I try to teach him how to do it for himself, but I know it will be easier when he is older, and of course, I'll do the same with my daughter as well.

Do it while someone is watching baby. Have the Dad, your Mom, your sister, or a trusted friend watch the baby for a couple of hours a week, just to get some meditation time in. Having this time, even once a week, will give you something to look forward to and space to clear your mind.

I find that I come up with great ideas and concepts in meditation that help me in being a better Mom. Perhaps an idea will come to mind about how to schedule or organize something which really helps me in the long run. Even if my mind is not completely blank the entire time, it is not a loss. This time is meant as a "pause" in your thinking. At first, your mind will run its course with thoughts of this and that, but eventually, with practice, you will find that "empty space" of bliss and love where you can remain for longer and longer periods. It takes time, which is something of a rarity with us Moms, but this is time well spent. Don't try for a lot of time at first; only do what you can. Meditating even once a week the first year is better than trying a couple of times the first week, then giving up.

For beginners, I always recommend guided meditation to start. You can find guided meditation CDs at your local library, any metaphysical store, or sometimes in or near the "World Music" section of your local music store. I particularly recommend Dr. Andrew Weil's "8 Meditations for Optimum Health" CD, as well as his "Meditation for Optimum Health" CD with Jon Kabat-Zinn, Ph.D.

Another fantastic guided meditation is the "Chopra Center 21-Day Meditation Challenge" by Deepak Chopra, at www. chopracentermeditation.com. These are very effective meditations because they are only 15 minutes and start out with a guided meditation, then silence, then guiding back.

After you're comfortable with guided meditation, my favorite CDs are by Steven Halpern; in particular "Chakra Suite," "Music for Sound Healing," and "Inner Peace," but you can't go wrong with any of his music. It's not just "meditation" or "relaxing" music, but considered "healing" music, because his particular skill is evoking tones that direct the brain to different alpha, delta, and theta waves for prime functioning ability. In particular, his "Brainwave Entrainment" CDs are cutting edge. Visit www.stevenhalpern. com for more information.

Pamper Yourself

THIS IS AN IMPORTANT one, albeit the hardest. Do what you can to pamper yourself. Make it a priority to take extra care of yourself during this time.

Ideally, however, you should schedule a monthly massage, "mani/pedi," or facial after Daddy gets home to just give yourself those few hours of luxury, and you won't have to pay a sitter. To finance it, hint to people to only give you spa certificates as birthday and Christmas gifts.

If spa time is not an option, try a walk in your local forest preserve or arboretum. Pure oxygen from the fresh air, trees, and plants will rejuvenate you.

You can do the simplest things without costing a dime. Taking just a minute to do some deep, calm stretching after a feeding or after returning home from a morning out with the kids will be beneficial. Try stretching every night before bedtime to alleviate the body's tensions from the day. After the kids are in bed, draw yourself a candlelit bath, play soft music, and/or bring a good book in the tub with you. Practice self-massage when the kids are napping or eating: Start from your head, working your way down to your neck, shoulders, lower back, calves, and feet. If you spend even five seconds on each part, that's only 30 seconds, but at least it's something! How about using a hot pack on your shoulders, back, or legs to relax while feeding baby? You can even soak your feet during this time. Get creative!

As Moms, we sometimes feel the idea of pampering ourselves is close to sacrilege because in the back of our minds we know we could be spending that money or that time on our children. Yet, it can't be said enough that "when Momma's happy, everyone's happy." You have an important job and you deserve (and need!) to take care of YOU – physically, mentally, and emotionally. The better you feel inside and out, the better you will be for your children.

Patience

THIS IS AN IMPORTANT trait to develop, more than in any other time in your life. Things will work themselves out eventually. Babies grow to become toddlers, toddlers grow to become school-age kids, school-age kids grow to become pre-teens, then teens, then adults. As it says in the Bible, "All things come to pass." Children grow and the situations that present themselves now will not last.

Given that, this is an opportunity to not only develop patience with your child(ren), but with yourself as well. The patience and coping skills you acquire now will carry you through anything and everything that comes up from this point forward.

As much patience as you give to your children, give to yourself. If you find it has run out, have the patience to forgive yourself and keep trying. It will only benefit you and your child(ren) all around.

I will always remember a story a friend of mine told that put things into perspective. She said she was angry that her son had made her 15 minutes late for their appointment that morning; however, between their home and the appointment she passed five car accidents. She had the presence of mind to recognize it was a blessing her son had made them late, as they could have been in any one of those accidents.

You just never know what the day will bring.

Positive Self-Talk

As A SAHM, you are all alone taking care of your baby(ies) all day long. Because we are Mothers, we are constantly making sure we have foremost in our minds all the things we need to do to care for and protect our children.

With babies, we think things like, "I have to make sure to be on time for the next feeding. I hope s/he is eating enough. When did s/he have a BM last? Is that normal? I wonder if s/he is growing properly?" We worry constantly.

If they are toddlers, we are mostly saying phrases like, "Stop!" "Don't touch that!" "Don't go there!" and "No!" and then (unless you are very lucky) you have the constant struggle with naptime and bedtime to deal with every single day, on top of continually picking up all the toys scattered all over the house.

Of course, we need to make sure our children are safe and well, but all that tension and negativity needs to be counteracted with positivity and thinking positive statements, or else we start to feel its effects in our minds and, subsequently, our bodies.

For me, it was even worse, because every time my child(ren) cried, I felt like a terrible Mom. I felt that perhaps I should just go back to work because obviously I wasn't doing a good enough job or my child would be happy and playing contently like I saw that he did in day care.

One day, I'd had enough of feeling bad and worrying. I decided to come up with better, more positive phrases to tell myself, and it really helped. Whenever I changed a diaper, I would think, "See, look how healthy my child is! His/her body is functioning perfectly, and I am feeding him/her just the right amount of food that they need." When I would play with them and laugh, I would think, "What a good Mom I am! My child is happy and playing harmoniously – this is what it's all about!"

When you are a new Mom, it is tough to do that, because you truly don't know what "normal" is yet, but you will. Until then, you have to trust your instincts and make the effort to educate yourself in any way possible, either by reaching out to other Moms or surfing the internet. There are dozens upon dozens of parenting websites out there with excellent information, but there is also such a thing as "information overload," so just be mindful of that as you research.

I trained myself to notice whenever I caught myself thinking something negative about my parenting, and then I stopped and tried to put a better spin on it. It wasn't easy, and I still slip, but practice makes perfect and you'll feel all the better for it. Basically, don't let your fears and worries eat at you and bring you down, because you need to be strong and a good role model for your children so that they have a sense that all is well. You know that you do your best and that anything you can do to make them happy, you will, and that whenever they are sick or unhappy, you'll be there to care for them to the very best of your ability.

When you get overwhelmed, try to keep perspective – remember, they will *never* be this young again; they will only grow and become more and more self-sufficient until the day comes you may wish they'd request something of you once more!

Be your biggest cheerleader and biggest fan. Whenever you accomplish even the littlest thing, be sure to acknowledge it and give yourself a pat on the back. You deserve it.

For example, when I had my little girl, it was a very rough transition for me going from one child to two, and especially because my son was a two-year-old and needed (and deserved!) copious amounts of attention, which was rather challenging. Therefore, to just learn to get them both dressed, bag packed, and out of the house in the morning to go anywhere was an enormous accomplishment for me. Some days I joke to myself, "Adrenaline and love...it's what gets me through the day!"

Unfortunately, anyone else who has never been home with little ones all day, every day, may not be understanding, supportive, sympathetic, or respectful to your situation. In my second book, *A Fish Out of Water*, I shared some personal accounts of situations where I was not supported and even looked down upon for my choice to stay at home with my children. Aside from what anyone else says or thinks, ultimately, you are the one talking to yourself inside your head all day, every day. You have to be the one to give yourself the respect, sympathy, understanding, and praise you deserve.

Remember Your Partner

TIME WITH YOUR HUSBAND/PARTNER/SIGNIFICANT Other is important to a new/young family unit and your sanity. Go to your list of sitters that hopefully you have created by now (suggested in the "Breaks" chapter), and see what you can do about creating a monthly "date night." If you are blessed enough to afford to hire a sitter, by all means do it.

If it is not in the budget to go out once a month, then try having a friend or relative watch the kids for just a few hours and have a "date night" right at home. Order in a pizza or Chinese food (so you don't have to cook), light some candles, put some music on, and you have yourself a romantic meal! Or if you're movie buffs like we are, rent a movie and pop some popcorn! The most important thing is that you two are alone. Ideally, it would be nice if you could talk and reconnect with each other, rather than spend hours in silence watching something, but you have to do what works for you.

Some experts say that during this time, you are not supposed to talk about the kids, but I think this could be the best time to do it, since perhaps you want to talk about things that you don't want them to hear, such as when to convert the crib to a bed, when to potty train, upcoming playdates or surprises for them, etc., and that is also a bonding experience between the two of you. If you are first-time parents, however, you probably would do well not to talk about the baby and just have a night out for dinner and wine! (If you are breastfeeding, just wait two hours per drink before feeding the baby.)

It is especially important to have constant, open communication between you and your husband/significant other when you are a SAHM. You two are living completely different lives now. Never take for granted he knows what's going on. The family calendar mentioned earlier helps with that.

Since you won't be able to be at the computer for constant e-mail communication, if you can get a phone that uses texts and gets e-mails, it would be ideal. Don't expect to be able to sit down and compose lengthy e-mails, but you will be able to text questions and comments to each other throughout the day to make sure you're both on the same page and let him know what's going on when possible.

I did this with my husband, but there were some days, mainly right after Victoria was born, that I couldn't even get to the phone to text him. However, when I can, it works great for us. I let him know the status on potty-training efforts, I call him when our son misses Daddy, and I take pictures of our baby standing and send to him – things like that are fun and useful.

Most importantly, however, the health of the relationship between you and your husband is of the utmost importance to the health of your family with little ones, and communication is at the core of all of it. When things are bad between you, the kids feel it and suffer. Being a new parent is the ultimate marriage-tester. Having kids can make or break a marriage. Do what you can to strengthen your relationship with your husband/significant other and make sure to make time for the two of you.

A happy marriage/partnership equals a happy home life. Do your best to avoid screaming, criticism, or judgment when it comes to communication between each other. Do what it takes to make sure you and your partner are even communicating at all (time alone together is a big factor in that). When you first become parents it can be such a shock to discover the chasm between your perception of "what it would be like" and the reality of "what it is actually like." You may discover thoughts and feelings you never thought you had, and he as well. Be honest and open with those thoughts and feelings, and be committed to working them out together.

Although becoming parents is a true relationship-tester, it can also be a relationship-strengthener as well, if you let it. You won't love him more than when you see him change his baby's diaper or play with his toddler. Yet, it is a heavy responsibility and toddlers have a way of pushing boundaries. Reach out for support by any means possible, but also keep in mind your partner needs support as well, and encourage him to get it. You can be each other's sounding board, but be careful not to turn into each other's whipping post.

One idea is to check into your insurance benefits and see what type of counseling or therapy services are available. I was fortunate enough to find we had four free sessions per year available for each of us to see a counselor/therapist. I chose to see a lady for my own stress management, and it was great for me to be able to talk to someone separate from the situation in order for me to be able to bounce ideas off of and for someone to listen who was unbiased. I highly recommend it for any parent, because helping yourself in this way also helps to strengthen your relationship, since being a parent can be very stressful for both of you. This way, you are "getting it out of your system" with your therapist and not just your husband/partner.

I also highly recommend couples' counseling. Having children, although a wonderful blessing, immediately changes the dynamic of your relationship and is an added stressor. New parents need help the most during this time, if only for a few months during the first year. Think of it as an investment in your marriage. Strengthening your foundation at this time of upheaval will secure you both for the rest of your life as parents and the ups and downs that lie ahead.

Take Care of Yourself

MAKE SURE YOU'VE GOT the basics down: Eat, sleep, shower, exercise, and drink plenty of water. I would get specific and say "Eat Right," but sometimes you have to work on remembering to eat at all!

All kidding aside, when you get to the point where you are eating regular meals, be mindful of what you are ingesting, especially if you are breastfeeding. Healthy foods and plenty of water make you feel better – it's as simple as that. Bonus: Eating raw veggies means no cooking time spent!

As far as exercise goes, that is a tricky one. If you just have a newborn, it is much easier to exercise because you can simply put him/her down in a bouncer or playpen, than it is in dealing with a toddler who is mobile and can get into all kinds of mischief while you're doing a workout video! So, it is best to begin/continue your exercise routine as soon as your doctor/midwife says it is okay after the birth. Have baby sleep in the bouncer or crib while you do the elliptical or treadmill (if you don't already have one, get a used one) or do workout videos. If the weather allows, go outside for a long walk with your baby in his/her stroller; or better yet, get a jogging stroller and go for a long jog.

For weight-bearing exercises, you can exercise with your baby. I would hold my baby and say, "William is going up-up-up!" while slowly lifting him up, then "William is going down-down-down!" and slowly bring him down (and I did the same with Victoria). This is a great arm workout! You can work your core by doing the same for twists as well; just lift your baby, tighten your abdomen and stomach muscles, then gently twist side-to-side. You don't want to do this exercise too vigorously, however, or you'll have a clean-up situation! Another fun one is to lay your baby below you on a soft rug or mat and do push-ups over him or her to teach "near" and "far." Websites like www.fitpregnancy.com have terrific ideas for exercising with your baby like this.

When my second child came along, my husband put a T.V. in the exercise room so my toddler could watch something educational (preferably, but not always the case!), while baby was in the bouncer. Also, we purchased a used double stroller from a friend that we used for family walks when my husband got home from work and on the weekends, weather permitting.

Now that the kids are three and one, they are a bit more interested in playing together, and thus, I have been successful in doing a "90-Day Challenge" via the Team Beachbody® Turbofire® program. This program only requires one hour a day, with one day rest during the week (meaning only one hour for six days a week) and one meal replacement shake. That was doable for me and it worked! I lost 16 pounds in 5 months. At first, the kids did interrupt, but eventually, they realized this was Mommy's workout time and played away from me on the other side of the room, so I had space to move around. They actually enjoyed watching the videos and listening to the music, and they even tried to do some of the exercises, too!

Sleeping was another big obstacle for me (as with all parents of little ones!) because I had my toddler's sleep schedule down, but when my newborn came along, that was all out the window, because their naps didn't coordinate. I was blessed enough to be able to have my Mom come over to watch when she could while I slept. One particularly bad night when the kids kept me up, my husband went in later to work just so I could have a few hours sleep. Sometimes, I'd just have to go upstairs and nap as soon as my husband came home from work. It was great when my daughter started sleeping through the night, but I still had a problem coordinating the afternoon naps. On the days that it worked out, I slept when they slept. Luckily, it got to a point where I was getting enough rest, but I just had to work it out like this until everyone was sleeping through the night regularly. It took a long time, but eventually it worked out.

Then, as my baby turned into a toddler and my toddler into a preschooler, they decided to get up multiple times during the night, and I had to start figuring out sleep remedies for them all over again! However, I know that this time is temporary and as I continue to work on getting them to sleep through the night, I know it won't be forever and I do my best to get to bed earlier as well. It worked out before, and it will work out again. I simply take the best care of myself that I can and do my best. Diligence is key!

Yoga for Mom

I FOUND IT WONDERFULLY helpful to sneak my yoga time in during "down time" moments. One example is when you are waiting for baby to fall asleep before going into your own bed. I would go all the way back to my bedroom, watch on the monitor, then if baby started crying, I'd wait the recommended five minutes, then go back. Eventually, I "graduated" to just waiting in the hallway. Realizing I actually had a few moments to do nothing but wait, I decided to be productive. So, instead of simply playing the back-and-forth game with baby, I used this time to do a simple yoga routine. (As stated in the previous "Meditation" chapter, I would meditate as well.)

In as little as five minutes, you can perform the sun salutation, butterfly, child's pose, snake, and several others. I did all those and even made up some of my own stretches that felt good to me as well.

Other times I find to sneak in yoga are when my toddler is doing "quiet time" activities, and when I am about to go to bed myself. I especially enjoy doing a simple routine at night before bed, because the stretching helps to alleviate and release the tensions from the day, as well as being an excellent precursor to meditation.

Conclusion

REMEMBERING GOD AND CENTERING yourself can be extremely hard being the parent of little ones who may fuss, cry, whine, argue, scream, and just about push every button you've ever had! I can clearly recall some emotionally difficult situations I've been in that drove me to self-reflect and connect with God just to get through the day. It's still tough. Some days are still more challenging than others. The difference between two years ago and today, is that I have this set of resources at my disposal for support. I could probably write a different book two years from now, as I learn more, but this is what I believe is true for me thus far, as I'm still living it.

Eventually, doing all of these things became a practice for me that I could depend on in good times and in bad. Therefore, I can now say those tough times had a silver lining in that I could create something tangible to help others in my predicament. It justifies whatever I went through if I could help others remember the constant Source of love and light that is there for us always – the reason we became parents in the first place.

May your journey on the path of parenthood bring you much joy and fulfillment!

Blessings and Namaste!

"Love makes us real"

- The Velveteen Rabbit by Margery Williams,
Published 1922

Appendix

Used with permission, here are some wonderful parenting affirmations from the September 2012, Volume 4, Issue 9, of the Holistic Mom's Network newsletter, "HealthE Mama News." Enjoy!

1. I trust my intuition.
2. I parent with love and respect.
3. My children are healthy and joyous.
4. Nurturing myself is essential to great parenting.
5. I am grateful for my children.
6. I try to share the joy and excitement of life through my child's eyes.
7. I give my child my full attention.
8. I let go of the difficult moments.
9. I have patience enough to handle all of my parenting challenges.
10. I love and respect my children as I respect myself.

Here are a few affirmations from the cards I created (front and back):

1. *I Am A Good Mother*
   I thoroughly enjoy being a Mother and I take comfort in the fact that I know I am doing the best I can. It is OK for me to continue learning and to make mistakes because I love my babies and I would never consciously hurt them. Every day I realize that being a Mom is getting easier and more enjoyable with each passing moment.

2. *I Am A Healthy, Happy Stay-At-Home Mom*
   I am happy being home with my children and can handle them with ease and grace, gentleness and patience, being calm and serene, clever and creative, resourceful and wise. Thank you, God!

3. *I Love My Family*
   I have a stable, calm, peaceful, happy home where we have wonderful food, cleanliness and orderliness, and abundant, relaxed, fun times with each other, extended family, and friends.

4. *My Children Are Divinely Protected*
   My children are divinely protected at every moment. I trust my instincts to know how to best care for them. I know that God brought them into this world for a reason, so I rest assured they have a divine purpose and are safe at all times in my presence and otherwise.

5. *I Find Balance*
   I experience the peace and personal fulfillment God brings, and I enjoy the simple things in life and all they have to offer.

Recommended Reading & Resources

Below are the titles of the children's books and CD's I have for my children. I hope you read and enjoy them with your tots as much as I did.

10 Big Ideas of New Thought Teaching for Kids 3-8 – Reverend Nancy Zala

Buddha at Bedtime: Tales of Love and Wisdom for You to Read With Your Child to Enchant, Enlighten, and Inspire – Dharmachari Nagaraja

Maybe: A Little Zen for Little Ones – Sanjay Nambiar

How to Remember Who You Are (Series) – Avianna Marie Jones, Ph.D.

I Am: Why Two Little Words Mean So Much – Dr. Wayne W. Dyer

I Think, I Am!: Teaching Kids the Power of Affirmations – Louise L. Hay and Kristina Tracy

Incredible You! 10 Ways to Let Your Greatness Shine Through – Dr. Wayne W. Dyer with Kristina Tracy

Indigo Ocean Dreams (CD) – Lori Lite

Just Imagine – John M. Thompson & George M. Schultz

One – Kathryn Otoshi

The Little Soul and the Sun – Neale Donald Walsch

Tiger-Tiger, Is It True?: Four Questions to Make You Smile Again – Byron Katie and Hans Wilhelm

The Twelve Gifts of Birth: A Message for Children of All Ages and the Child in Every Adult – Charlene Costanzo

We Are Love – Jennifer Black

What I Believe – Jennifer Murphy-Morrical

You Are A Gift To The World / The World Is A Gift To You (A Flip-Sided Book...Like Love it Never Ends) – Laura Duksta

Most titles available on www.amazon.com, or visit www.hayhouse.com, www.cwg.org, www.conversationswithgod.org, and www.devorss.com for more children's titles.

Other Publications:

Awakenings – Shakti Gawain

Celebrating the Great Mother: A Handbook of Earth-Honoring Activities for Parents and Children – Cait Johnson and Maura D. Shaw

Organic Housekeeping: In Which the Non-Toxic Avenger Shows You How to Improve Your Health and That of Your Family While You Save Time, Money, and Perhaps Your Sanity – Ellen Sandbeck

"Science of Mind" Magazine – www.scienceofmind.com

Spontaneous Healing: How to Discover and Embrace Your Body's Natural Ability to Maintain and Heal Itself – Dr. Andrew Weil

Meditation CD's:

8 Meditations for Optimum Health – Dr. Andrew Weil
Meditation for Optimum Health – Dr. Andrew Weil with Jon Kabat-Zinn, Ph.D., www.drweil.com

Chakra Suite – Steven Halpern
Inner Peace – Steven Halpern
Music for Sound Healing – Steven Halpern, www.stevenhalpern.com

Meditations for Manifesting – Dr. Wayne W. Dyer

Lecture CD's:

101 Power Thoughts for Life – Louise Hay
Embracing Change – Louise Hay, www.louisehay.com

Abundance for Life (Program) – Paul Scheele,
www.learningstrategies.com/AbundanceForLife/Home.asp

The Essence of Being in Balance – Dr. Wayne W. Dyer
Inspirational Thoughts – Dr. Wayne W. Dyer
The Keys to Higher Awareness – Dr. Wayne W. Dyer
The Wayne W. Dyer CD Audio Collection – Dr. Wayne W. Dyer,
www.drwaynedyer.com

Nightingale Conant Audio CDs – www.nightingale.com

Sounds True Audio CDs – www.soundstrue.com

Websites:

Dances for Universal Peace, www.dancesofuniversalpeace.org

Drumming Circle (Kid Friendly) – Darlene Palese, www.meetup.
com/WeDrumSheDrums

Green Housecleaning – About.com

Holistic Moms Network – www.holisticmoms.org

How To Remember Who You Are – www.howtorememberwhoyouare.com

Labyrinth – Theosophical Society, www.theosophical.org

Labyrinth and Children's Labyrinth Products –
Relax4Life Center, www.relax4life.com

Meetup – www.meetup.com

Mindful Living – www.earth911.com

Music Together – www.musictogether.com

One Spirit Book Club – www.onespirit.com

Team Beachbody – www.teambeachbody.com

Card Decks:

Inspiration: Your Ultimate Calling – Dr. Wayne W. Dyer

The Original Angel Cards – Kathy Tyler and Joy Drake

Power Thought Cards – Louise L. Hay

Words of Wisdom – His Holiness the Dalai Lama

Miscellaneous:

DuPage Center for Spiritual Living – www.dupagecenter.org

Intention & Blessing Circles and Remote Work – www.agangofgirls.com